MISTER SKYLIGHT

MISTER SKYLIGHT
ED SKOOG

COPPER CANYON PRESS

PORT TOWNSEND, WASHINGTON

Cover art: Michel Varisco, *Open Window,* from the "Ruminations" series, 2004. Silver gelatin print, 16 x 20 inches.

Copper Canyon Press is in residence at Fort Worden State Park in Port Townsend, Washington, under the auspices of Centrum. Centrum is a gathering place for artists and creative thinkers from around the world, students of all ages and backgrounds, and audiences seeking extraordinary cultural enrichment.

LIBRARY OF CONGRESS CATALOGING-IN-PUBLICATION DATA

Skoog, Ed.
  Mister Skylight / Ed Skoog.
    p. cm.
  ISBN 978-1-55659-293-5 (pbk. : alk. paper)
  I. Title.

PS3619.K66M57 2009
811'.6—dc22

2009009362

98765432 first printing

COPPER CANYON PRESS
Post Office Box 271
Port Townsend, Washington 98368
www.coppercanyonpress.org

Acknowledgments

I wish to thank my family and these readers, whose attention helped create this book: Ben Lerner, Catherine Barnett, James Hoch, G.C. Waldrep, Anne Gisleson, Andy Young, Brad Richard, Derick Burleson, J. Robert Lennon, Nick Twemlow, Carolyn Hembree, Eric McHenry, T.R. Johnson, Jarret Lofstead, Peter Cooley, Chris Chambers, Michael Collier, Brad Leithauser, X.J. Kennedy, Elizabeth Scanlon, Rhian Ellis, Andy Greer, David Gilbert, Alex Speyer, Kurt Slauson, A.J. Rathbun, Jeremy Holt, Mark Lane, Elizabeth Urschel, Joseph Bednarik, Jessica Rice, and Michael Wiegers.

Grateful acknowledgment is made to the following publications, in which these poems first appeared: *American Poetry Review:* "Like Night Catching Jackrabbits in Its Barbed Wire," "Memory Loss"; *City Arts:* "And the Yellow Bones of the Parking Lot"; *Louisiana Literature:* "Canzoniere of Late July"; *Naked Punch:* "The Santa Fe *Chief*"; *Narrative:* "West Coast"; *New Orleans Review:* "Season Finale"; *NO:* "Pilgrim: An Ode"; *Paris Review:* "Inland Empire" as "October"; *Ploughshares:* "Ruler of My Heart"; *Poetry:* "Home at Thirty," "The Carolers"; *Practice:* "Help in Seven Languages Written on the Skeleton Coast"; *Slate:* "Autobiographical"; *The Double Dealer:* part of "Party at the Dump" as "Grand Isle is Sinking"; and *Threepenny Review:* "During the War." Sections of "Punks Not Dead" appeared, under different titles, in *CutBank, Sonora Review,* and *Third Coast.* Sections of "Mister Skylight" appeared, under different titles, in *Horn Gallery, Marlboro Review, Forklift Ohio, The Canary, failbetter.com, Barrow Street, LitRag, Fourteen Hills, Sidebrow, Indiana Review,* and *The New Republic.*

"The Carolers" has also appeared in *Poetry Daily* and the alt.NPR program *Poetry Off the Shelf,* hosted by Curtis Fox.

Contents

for Jill

MISTER SKYLIGHT

During the War

I lived in two houses, one apartment,
took notes on a cocktail napkin
and a record store receipt my salary
almost covered. I abandoned my longing
to be more serious, and grew out my hair.
Summer, I shaved to bury my mother,
mourned a full season on the couch,
television bright across shag carpet.

The train I rode around America
was empty; the country was half-empty,
like the zoo on Monday. I wept at the president,
threatened to barefoot across the border,
but in the end only rolled down the window
to wave at a stranger who looked familiar.

I

Ruler of My Heart

Halfway through the first
song I catch her, Irma
Thomas bringing the station
back from storm and flood,
singing in slow 6/8
I've had enough. I
know she means
she also doesn't know
what secret sent every quarter
down Markey's jukebox.
"Robber of my soul,"
she calls, and now
in the gradual blue
we beg you to come back,
gold and breathing,
who never goes away.

Season Finale

My last look around the house
took so long that the vine
climbing the rosebush climbed
into my eyes, and a lizard
climbed, too, mouthfirst from grass,
its skin changing color
from grass green to a green
almost without green,
the color of dust on feather.
How changed from last winter's
midnight when I let the dog out
and rats ran from the mimosa
to the fence while shingles
sparkled on the lawnmower shed,
and in the grass, a cold lizard
raised a claw. How changed
from the next week's water
writing its black line across plaster
I cannot read in California,
where I hold the cellphone hot
while Lofstead, early returner,
kicks the back door in
to tell me of the damage.
Images come fast to the small,
impersonal screen,
linoleum sandy and streaked,
walls dice-dotted with mold,
and through a broken window,
the rosebush ash-gray, the yard
ash-gray and without lizard.

Party at the Dump

What can't be seen under the thrown
was home. The sky and its turbulent guard
fresco the kestrel storm harmless and east,
arrive like a hostage, an ear, a finger in the mail.
Wind unhooks the mirliton vine, kisses each begonia.
Shadow bricks the window shy. Cups fly.
There are times one ought to charge or fall back.
What I win from masking-tape tic-tac-toe
on the bedroom's nine windowpanes,
I spend in silver, spend in empty hallway.
No one's my brother tonight, watering his lawn.
So I take my chair to the roof flat as the hour.
Wind hangs laundry on the gable.
The hour is suitcase and landmine.
The moon rises over the abandoned town
like cutlery on the high shelf.
Our fishing camp is hip-deep now,
at the end of tidal song. Westbank cattle swim
to the east bank, and wind turns wood
in high cello. Sunset ripens and ruptures.
If I were nothing I'd be home by now
in Hemet, or Anza, or Los Angeles,
below the moon's IV drip. From the pueblo
of the anesthesiologist and soup spoon
there is some wandering up. No one there is
my brother watering his lawn, and he calls
to see how I'm doing. And this is where I start,
at Mr. Samuel's Tire Shop on St. Claude Avenue.
Life must be worth something
for the loss of it to hurt so much.
Take the foreign policy of weather,
palmetto bugs caravanning up the lime tree.

Winds crater power lines, and from these,
an empty and alone beauty busters down,
bullies the shotgun house, keeps a body
up late. Dogs know, the wild ones,
wheel-scarred and healed, that the storm
brings from hiding to scratch a deaf ear,
to sneak short lifelong sneaks brave to live:
I know the secret is to stay low,
adventure between calendar and heart.
Today's hurricane flag only waves in photos.
The ocean opens Grand Isle like a casket.
We hit the beach late, dimple blanket
beside the fishing pier, where children seal,
spell with sparklers the Fourth of July.
Roman candles fire green artillery into the sea.
Teenagers park, sneak through scrub
to beach, and burn driftwood distinctions
between lie, lay, lain. My interest
is in things that disappear, ten men in dark
jackets staring asea, some foreign orchestra.
Is that you in the seat ahead of me?
You've never been here before.
This frog comes halfway in the open door
of Butler's Bar and Restaurant. So it must be
frog time. Saturday night scouring levees down
into the gutters of Tchoupitoulas.
Then it's Sunday and I'm at your doorstep.
Between Mr. Samuel's and the cop garage:
water. As a kid, I knew the magic show
was a shape of eternity. And somewhere else
the desert smells like fresh belts and sweetly
tries to take us down. We went to look at what
was being forged, a quarrel in the mountains,
sketchbook avalanches covering up the world

and its passports, any business what the mountain does.
Hostages wash up at the embassy, unharmed.
Seven days after the storm those who did not want
to leave, or did, find ground in the laughter of loss.
When the wind turns along the fence, when the gray
horse rounds the turn, blue arguments gnarl
podiums of sky. Wind kneels its August februation.
The boy with the web painted on his face
pursues his thoughts through the vineyard.

Help in Seven Languages Written on the Skeleton Coast

On the Skeleton Coast the hard knots
wash up and are buried,
unburied. Endured.
No one resolves to untie them
with massive, piglike hands
that hold up sails, lugging together
fables of capital and labor
in futtock shroud.
Knots have names, faces.

Knots bear themselves forward.
On the Skeleton Coast lie preserved
words for help in seven languages
in stones above high-tide line,
but twelve skeletons lined up,
unpronounceable silken words,
remain from earlier encounterings.
Some knots bob like seals past the breakers.
Is the other end tied to something.

Some states decommission their asylums,
embourgeoisent the chambers into condominiums.
One buyer, asked about the "creepiness factor,"
(I heard on the radio just now) said
"Some things are real, some things ain't."
Meanwhile, Cindy still sleeps nude
in the apartment overlooking the river,
and old people talk about each other.
My students find, in hallways, love;

next-door children find toys in the forest
and break them. Try looking under the porch.
None have looked for what they've lost

on the Skeleton Coast of Namibia,
though some seek other coasts
whose dunes may also render
skeleton or a knot, or bottle of Woolite,
white Venus dislodged from shrine.

Lions bash into the water after a whale.
A beetle drifts. All departures: canceled.
They endure themselves to fang and consider.
Eroded by water and sand, I hide discarded,
down to sea: this Skeleton Coast elephant
visiting at first, then devoured from the mouth.
Waiting in shifts to exit, we follow the dry riverbed
to escape the Skeleton Coast until bones sit up,
waking, grin no gold, no, a sheer goldlessness

as if saying I want to understand "dead,"
this "nothing." Nothing for breakfast.
I'm dead tired, where's the washroom.
Namibia: *namib:* no-place place *never*—
the difference between honey and molasses,
under a skeleton cloud in moonlight.
Tusks clash tonight
yards from foam between tides.
You hear it. You do not hear it.

Memory Loss

When I write
"the pigeon is large or rubied or hungry"
it is because we used to haul finished cabinets
to the factory's dark hot second floor
up a shabby freight elevator,
and at the bottom of the elevator shaft
corpses of a few pigeons
continued in feathers
beside broken wine bottles, leaves, pooled oil.

I write it because we are in the dark,
years later, and I want to tell you

how I had to pass by the elevator
to the break room, impatient for midnight,
when my shift would end and Kevin,
having also finished his workday
clerking at the Kwik Shop, would pull
his golden Opel into the loading dock
and we'd drive around Topeka, listening
to James Brown's *Everybody's Doin' the
Hustle & Dead on the Double Bump*,
windows rolled laboriously down,

but every time I passed the elevator
and looked down into the pit, I had
to acknowledge the skeletal wings
and blank eyes that would never revive,

not even from the obscure forest of memory,
fly to the forefront of my brain
where it perches, looks with black eye
into mine, and ruffles its chest.

When I write "I forgot my silencer"
I mean I have forgotten my silence,
and would like to be thought of
as a dangerous person,
as someone who is intriguing

rather than a teenager again
wandering the stoned aisles of the summer market.
So when I write "starved tigers devour us
with an uncomfortable vitality"
I am thinking about all the people I've lost,
those torn, shredded, fouled, and swallowed
by the eagerness of car crash, cancer, stroke, old age, youth,
        money, anger, love,
distance, madness.

*

O'Neal ran the Saturn Bar. His heart called last call a few
months after the flood, and in my fever he raises his shirt, a
pale guyaberra, to show the scar at a party, and he serves a
blue drink in a flower vase, and one for himself. Soon the host
kicks us to the gum-blackened curb. The black van covered in
S&H Green Stamps screeches tires and begins shooting to re-
claim O'Neal and take me, too. We run, leap lawns, are di-
vided. I scale a treehouse, hide for days until the backyard
party below me starts climbing up with hideous gloves. My
fever should have been a prose poem, an entity separated out
and managed in its own tradition rather than asking to find a
place here. They almost reach me. I look up and see blue gels
from theater lights fluttering, caught in cottonwood branches.

*

"Sun limps down the insecticide road"
is self-explanatory, in a country way.

"Stenciled memos that cover
windows of the new biowarfare wing"
are the same memos you probably got.
Check your e-mail. They were so
numerous we had to use them
in place of curtains, or in place of currency,
and then, when we ran out of curtains,
as curtains. I wrote "the yellow crane whirs"
because they keep building things
where the obscure forest used to be,
and partly is, and I left my car at the trailhead
where the arborist writes her notes.

Oranges shine down on the kid bored
of churches, hungry for sweet gum a peso brings
from the round machine. Church, gum,
and auto parts store are yellow. The interior
is a food fight built from human surfaces,
while we swing open doors of wet, blue paint
on earthquake cracks, ferns feathering out.
Whatever we done was did because it might,
and bronzely bright in the courtyard's wire chair
delicately accepting cigarettes, you throw out
ice cream, look home, wig out on the morning ride,
attentive as trumpeter swans. I wash up behind the saint.
I'm sorry if this is ruining anything.
Every morning I wake civilization up
tight in its filthy sleeping bag. It rolls
back slumbering, later limps to bathroom
mirror and disappoints what it sees. Oh this
is what I am. Newspapers roll up
indecipherable. Fireworks puff
above the cell tower, the fountain where
rhododendrons develop next year's narrations.

The watertower drips. Speed bump paint is wet.
I have forgotten my silencer, and wait
outside the restaurant in San Bernardino
where inside I am writing notes
toward the poem I will abandon
under unused clouds, with ultimately
unused coupons clipped under wiper blades.

There's a guy who installs car stereos inexpertly
and I appreciate what little craftsmanship
he does have, at the lonely outpost, a hut
shaped like a camera from its previous life
as a one-hour-photo, which, like
this poem's previous life, kept its leftover
unclaimed images in a cardboard box
and is obscene, blurry, and/or both.

*

I return the execution video
because of all the execution videos
I would rather have not seen,
a selfish act on one hand
because executions happen
without my watching them,
but now the dead return
in dreams, unseen.

I show this poem to my grave,
which suggests I not write "down the road
and down the hill," and wants,
insofar as the grave *wants,*
more specificity about what kind of car,
and I say Taurus. So lean
against your Taurus and my grave asks

what kind of tree? Pine.
So a woman goes walking in pines,
and gets disoriented. Her grin steps from posters
stapled to telephone poles (which were pine).

Into estuary moonlight the whale
wanders and now the broken study
of its organs accuses no one
from underneath some towels.
This is what we have to work with.

Cholula, July 2007

Home at Thirty

On the street at midnight, I hear
a hatbox latch fall open
in an attic closet, and then
the silence of Alexandria.

Even low clouds' dark stucco seems
applied by the drowsiest journeyman.

The fire hydrant stares
from its tricolor at a branch
fallen in the street.

A snail punches antennae up the chain,
a great excursion to the loose
bolt where a little water drips.

The Carolers

in scarf and boot turn
around our neighbor's pine,
spill grog into snow,
approaching our porch with
"O Come All Ye Faithful."
A few stumble or sing wrong,
open the door, Jim for
come let us adore him.
Annual Christian, pipered
by their pied joy, I lean
to follow when they go.
A hand holds me back.
The lead caroler, encountering
our Ford glazed with ice,
undeterred, opens the door
and crawls right through,
knees on the seat, gloves
on the dash and headrest.
The rest follow, pulling
"I Saw Three Ships"
through the car like a rope.
Soon I am falling asleep
in vast winter bedroom silence,
and I am singing with them
through local traffic
houses towns lives
exile and years of night.

Early Kansas Impressionists

Silly now, when she visits
dreams, or I visit her, my mother,
in new condos at belief's edge
where the neon restaurant's lawn
shallows with winter. She laughs
in the expanse, wordless, collapsing
into snow to wave arms and legs,
craft a figure. I do the same,
like an infant learning its body.
Dusting off, I rise and she's gone
every time. I see our shapes
then, mine a mimicry of myself,
hers a rectangular silence,
inhuman, without room
for rage shame guilt or scold,
the curves that let us recognize
each other in the air, O,
in our dynamic world today.

The Kansas River, Also Called Kaw

We go about stabbing Larry O'Neal
six blocks from river's knife
while neon sings from the taco joint
and used records mutter, in plastic,
the slap I earn for singing names,
not just Larry but the rest of dead Topeka:
Sam Eisland, Nikki Mendoza, Bruce Whaley,
Randy Ijams, dead and black and my age
tied to rails by the Kansas River,
rope forgotten in great desegregation.
Shawnee County binds his arms and ankles,
as boxcars ballast, rock rails held in steel.

In another early death, midnight's Cadillac
wrecks on the traffic circle, and I,
out walking, run to address the damage.
A cop asks *why are you in the car?* I'm not,
I'm not. I'm in the blond kid's basement
dashing all the spices into a jelly jar,
celery salt, mace, curry, bay, a potion
we dare each other drink, tongue-disgusted,
yet go upstairs changed by countertop erotics.
Topeka's grand opening never happens.
Bison wander the unpalleted limestone.
A padlock holds Boyle's Joyland closed

where I ride the tilt-a-whirl again, spin
safe in canvas straps as faces blend.
Iron belt clanks in the turning. Leaning
into the tobacco of a stranger's sleeve,
I let my cap fly, and it lands blue beyond
the shaking rails among the fallen change.
Skee-ball tickets kiss with red tongue

the clarinet music closing magenta
over our eyelids as bumper cars crash
beside the river, leaves fall, tilt, whirl
on the surface, the surface that carries us
with uncertain carriage, seasonal, and thin.

Punks Not Dead

The eye is inmate in the head of error,
another animal entirely, which saw
anonymous fists come out of the crowd
because the mouth was busy talking so much,
a magnificent buzz of being that meantime
is not felt down the corridor,
where a black eye stares into itself
in the mirror above the ceramic sink.
The eye, hamstrung by the rest of the body,
seer and recorder, dizzies from conflict.

Racing around the room to take down what is,
as much what it sees as what it is,
the punched eye becomes a church, a thing
surrounded by bruised earth, and so far
as *that* goes, styptic graves near churches are
escape nor solution. The shovels you step on
to loosen sod are, like words, drawn to graves,
to trying out what may work yet knotting into
another element always. The digger chews
spearmint gum. His thoughts gadabout

past the shack they keep lawnmowers in,
past sight into amphetamine blue haze
where sky beneath horizon slips its blade;
he digs for hours, mind astringent, pea
jacket pocket flapping, cemetery
cedars turning red to dark. Dig. Dig.
I go into crowds, hoping for riot, and know
a crowd is an amalgam of the general crush,
like prison or epic. I go into a crowd's ontogeny,
mark the move from grown to embryo.

Going into crowds, I hope a tyro will tutor me
in what's still young, show new divisions preening,
subscribers to an abstract cool. In the crowd,
eyes dart from dirt to rain, picking out
which brawlers will start the fight, who presides,
lead starling in a long scarf of starlings
wrapping itself around a river, flying tories,
which gang plans a dinner table fire.
In crowds are islands that seem oases,
asteroidal revolutionaries.

I go into crowds to learn how to move
many as one, the latest tatting pattern
of bones going into the body, occipital
tori, the many tendons of the wrist.
Groups in the crowd are covered in sores.
Inside the gala of ribs the salsa of organs
moves like featured performers in red,
riot of longing under mama's belly,
or saw through the gamma broadcast
clipped to the doctor's light, curled bones,

fetal catafalque, each facet and cleft
fleshed out by the doctor's pen,
the one skeleton projecting us trying to remain
parental to this white sketch against black
faucet, a claque to fawn it into morning.
And at the base of the x-rayed neck a solarium
glows warm, the neckbones concatenating,
woven around a sucked thumb that may
taste like sourballs, the kid's wince
transfers to transparency.

There may be something valuable in thumbs.
They are crowded into so many mouths,
cedilla for the chin, ladled by a fist.

You have to ask, what was your war crime?
This is social work, walking around,
wanting to tell the woman who left hours ago
that her scarf still lies across the bench.
At the end of the world one feels worldlier.
Perhaps one should: but not in the locker room,
sneaking past untouchable versions of ourselves.

Jesuits play three-on-three with nuns
every other noon. Behind a pane
of wire-glass the dude in charge whistles
that worrisome cosmology that says
we may, when we shuck our worm garb,
walk aisles of our own, only nodding
solemn to amigos when we should be rollicking.
And behind the body, there isn't very much.
Blood is made of single things. I've seen photos.
Serological oarsmen row our veins.

We were all some sort of hod-carriers, then.
Felt good to hate you first, in the aisle,
surveillance mirror shining down an image
of long angry line where I stand,
for nothing, beside the usual magazines:
"my era" described, *Slanted and Enchanted*
ten years released to stores, my time machine
bringing back those small, unclean apartments,
where I pressed play on the stereo and waited.
At the end of the world, you feel the steel sides.

What the hands were doing they did in synch
with feet. O sweet the hips. The hammer angles
into the other morning maths. I hear it
through plywood, through drywall. Burdensome dance.
Roll up the steps in some hobo bindle

and stroll. A dance of curving, cotton slacks,
thrift-store T-shirt dancing bad as you.
Nails pierce the boards and the attic sharpens.
Hey. I was supposed to have beaten
the whoopee out of you. Cadres of the vanguard,

corps, and squads pass beneath my iron window,
where perched hummingbirds fresh from enjambed
cotillions stomp, almost making them leave—
hey—the world's deserted. Building and billboards
appear drawn by a drowsy cartoonist.
If Henri Michaux rolled by on skateboard,
the sound of his four green wheels would have
the whole block to resound in. No boards roll.
This house has left no people split-level, vacant.
What objects sat for ceremony stay undisturbed.

Now some people have returned to read.
One busload spools around the traffic circle.
Others follow on horseback, on parachute.
A slow reinvasion, then. Apartment windows
advent open. Cars load interstate and shrink
toward destination. Neighbors coffee-cake.
When will familiar bats or black birds fly
from heavy rhododendrons?
A short train ride and there's the sea,
slapping the shore with white hands.

The Santa Fe *Chief*

Speaking to no one, not being spoken to,
I listen to the desert's deposition, silent
argument from a jealous place. I sleep
upstairs. Trestles shake the stars.
I fall in love hourly, recall in doze
a lover's sweaty hair, the narrative particular.
She's in each overgrown backyard we pass,
by a baseball field that stays lit all night
and fresh cement drying on a wall.

Our young Marine in blue reflection
exposes his tattoo, a skull, a rose,
then tapes back up the bandage they gave him.
Stink of the traveler: armpit scraggle,
the rash, the breath, the discolored underwear.
Reading in the narrow Amtrak stairway,
the clerk drags his beard across the page
until the lounge attendant gets off work
to share a joint beside the suitcase rack.

We standby an hour in Albuquerque.
I walk around and say my morning prayer
past a blanket folded on a folding table.
The train, seen wholly from an overpass,
stays silver in its servicing. Downtown
the people wander in and out of doors.
Their bank clock spins too fast and makes me late.
I run the last block waving to the clerk
who holds the yellow stoop up to his vest.

Canzoniere of Late July

Almonds drop and temple the soil.
Carrots grow longways into earth.
The Mississippi carries clouds of soil
in gigantic purling. Winds erode soil,
making it savage to live above dirt,
always shifting. Listen as whispering soil
becomes a tropical opera of soil.
My immigrants build houses of sod
prairie afternoons, bury one another in sod
winter afternoons when snow covers soil
hard to farm, plowing between stones.
So, in my sleep tonight, there are these stones.

They roust me from bed and I panic my soul
caught on the nail of a drainpipe all night
outside my window. Slipped away, my soul
becomes my shadow; unshadowed by soul
I wander around card-house obligations,
find a broom, step to rescue my soul
hanging there like overalls, shoulder to sole,
and when I lift it with broom, my body
feels washed in a bath. Mimicking, bawdy,
five sensations tingle through my soul,
remember the plunge to which flesh belongs,
the scare to which it also belongs.

We stay up all night, sort of dancing
to the terror radio. At dawn I dress
and continue into daylight our dancing
steps into downtown's thousands dancing
between bus stops and jobs, man's seven stages
tumbling one before the other. Square dancing
follows feet; the shoulder leads slam dancing

to the invisible and everywhere-beaten drum.
The body's designed for persuasion by drum.
The soul's beaten. Reflections are dancing
although the drumset's mute, the scaled guitar
plays nothing, nor the acoustic guitar

hanging from its nail. The sidewalks
where dancers wear suits of flax and wool
are not dancing, and an iguana slowly walks
on stones of ruined city sidewalks,
contentedly licking its chops, and it goes on
with sideways gait where builders took walks
to admire pyramids, the way Ray Charles walks
hot streets of New Orleans at dawn
cracking up but the cracking dawn
belongs to him now, not to nighthawks
winging back to boardinghouse beds they made,
smoothing away proof of the love they made.

The CD skips a track, an LP album's turned,
the cassette tape unspools in its car stereo deck,
and all the songs danced to are turned
unrecognizable, and in traffic heads are turned
in brief confusion at melodies unexpected.
By the time the needle's dusted and returned
to the only song I want to hear, the song's turned
against me, no longer soothes, as if a thread
of pleasure's been dropped, the looping thread
I'd need to navigate the maze turned
to the map all travelers have to oblivion,
as if guidebooks could rescue from oblivion

anyone who can be knocked down with stones
thrown in anxious defense of soil.
Some break in half. Geodes are less stones

than papayas, and the papaya seeds of stones,
chewed and spat on a bare spot of earth,
grow as we watch them into larger stones,
generations later become more than stones,
push beyond the easy gravities of dirt.
I would rather push a wheelbarrow of dirt
than take the heavy pick to stones,
or rebuild a frontier church of sod,
though some the arduous way have sought;

but could conjecture forget what belongs
of body to the permanent sod of my soul?
Not hip bone hooked where leg bone belongs,
but when part of the substance I could be longs
to merge with the spinached narrows of midnight,
could I lose sense of where my soul belongs?
Bargain doubt of where my soul belongs?
If I let midnight ringtone my obligations
of breath and love, and replace obligations
with worm or flame, will I forget what belongs
to those with claim to my name and body,
obligated to breathe, love, bury my body

under prairie suffering? I've tried to learn guitar,
to make my fingers fall into that dancing.
The harder I force, more they forget. Are
there instant powders for instilling guitar
skill for sale from women in regional dress
at some voodoo crossroads? Picking guitar,
I can strum the chords in *Let's Learn Guitar,*
G, C, and D7, in garage; but up on stage,
my back would be against the wall of the stage.
I'd go shoegazer, and they'd yank the guitar
from my hands and make me bang the drum.
Red alert. Storm brewing. Alarmed by drum,

estuarine communities say prayers to who made
them eat mangrove; go on long mean walks
to hunt bushmeat; colonial ancestors who made
tactical mistakes. I often leave the bed unmade,
forget to pull tartan blanket weaved from wool
tight across the mattress the mattress factory made
and Mom had delivered to our door made
from an oak tree that could no longer go on
while the demand for front doors would go on.
And all the creatures that jug-band in the shade
have to find a new shade to hide in at dawn.
Ray Charles's sleeves grow damp at dawn.

A potter I know knows about oblivion.
For every decorative dish she's turned
on her heel and sent to the possible oblivion
of the kiln, she's had to forget oblivion.
She presses sign into clay, so when the deck
her products rest on decomposes into oblivion,
her sign will become part of oblivion;
in some geologic time nobody has expected,
future diggers will strike the unexpected
shards and have to contemplate oblivion
the way she did, that knotted thread
that through the centuries' eyes may thread,

so let the Maya build without sod
more pyramids from Yucatecan stones.
The old ones have been covered with sod.
(And cover the rebuilt ones again with sod.)
Let astronauts terrafirm alien soil
for pioneers to condition their fear of sod
away from where pioneers have divorced sod.
For I'm tired of studying only this Earth,
happy and unhappy families scarring the earth,

and want to expand past the mysteries of sod,
ramble around on something not called dirt.
As dirt extinguishes me, let me extinguish dirt.

It twists in the wind. Soul spoke to body:
inhale whatever mists, to what they belong,
burl the random stones of wordless body,
dream to tour thighs of a nectarine body.
Even if I knock, it's not kick of soul
gestating within, but a new set of obligations.
Possession sets its own obligations.
It can be argued that it never ends, night,
the way sun has to break it. The default is night.
Night renders to day, often, a dead body,
renders like a trawler a maw of obligations
not to shrimp, but to the shrimp boat obligations,

slick jackets backed against the oil drum,
and each eye the black hole of a guitar.
On the river, I hear the war drum
in every birdcall. The early radio's *all* drum,
and the nightmare cartoon keeps dancing
to some inner unstoppable drum
of mine, which evolves the body into a drum,
skin stretched tight as the dancer's dress
at some nightclub going on without address,
with all my lovers playing drum
up on the crepe paper and bunting of the stage,
until I'm summoned to appear onstage.

What seems staged, emerging from dawn
solid as last night's settling dusk made
seem knock the harsh scenery of dawn,
rosy cutout fingers from classical dawn,
millifleur yards where the gardener walks,

first one awake. He sprays on the dawn
nutrients and poisons so the next dawn
may urge aubades from bards with wool
cloaks drawn down over their pallid wool-
white visages. In red pajamas on the lawn
I walk to allow the project to go on.
Morning wears hardest: I can't go on.

Centuries are not made of thread,
but I don't know what they, or oblivion,
are made of, sugarplums and, if any thread,
red and black of licorice. Pull sweater thread
and see how the equator has always turned,
like a top, though more fuse than thread;
centuries are not made from simple thread,
but of hours drying on the lakehouse deck.
Straps of swimwear lace the deck.
Fate's rigged with rope, not thread.
Death's kiss tastes ripe plum: unexpected.
Flamenco plays behind the arras, unexpected.

Is it sufficient to believe in dirt?
The mind will join eventually with sod,
merging memory of a lovely kiss with dirt
and its caress; the hands I wash dirt
from will become cleansed of hands. Stones
are mountain range and pebble and dirt.
Would the king would sign a treaty with dirt,
a truce to let dirt stay dirt, soil
soil, and my body can stay above soil,
keep sweeping, from kitchen floors, dirt.
No more watching my heart disappear in earth.
Then it would be worth staying put on Earth,

worth obeying the animal obligations,
worth the butchery to feed the body
at the dinner table. Shun your obligations
and others will abandon their obligations.
Part of the sky decides what belongs
to the body. Fate is what's next. Obligations
presume an obligator. If my obligations
wake up soon and live with you, soul,
then what contract? Who souls the soul?
At the beach, one loses obligations.
The hatchet gets sharpened at night.
Moths trade candleflame for moonlight?

Leather heels mash my name into the stage.
Bending my body back to the drum
means what it looks like. The stage
is not sufficient to contain all the stages
of my play-grief, exaggerated by guitar.
But real grief is relayed here, too, on stage.
My soul's red dress spins across the stage,
means that not only my body is dancing.
Everything dead and alive is also dancing.
The entire world is only *this* stage,
these boards swept clean by my dress.
As the dance goes on, you'd think I'd undress.

Bring my backstage robe. Sorry, I can't go on
with my act. Help me limp back, Dawn,
ignore the audience's terror, let them go on
chanting and screaming for me to go on.
The time I saw him, James Brown made
it almost to the edge of the stage. "Can't go on!"
His agony was our air. But then he *could* go on.
Rejecting his robe, he ran because nobody walks

to the microphone when the spirit walks
within each vein that formerly couldn't go on.
The robe he lets fall, five more times, is wool.
Audience produces a green wool.

Vision ends, but even this is not unexpected,
because the eyes seem woven from iron thread.
Snowman of plums in a bowl can be unexpected,
tart skin breaking under tooth: unexpected,
like any small kindness faced with oblivion,
a proposition. This is when the unexpected
tears entreaties, citing conflicts unexpected.
Punches in diplomatic pouches are returned,
and hopes for a blue-sky solution are turned
to sorrow. Regroup when time unexpected
grants us leave to stretch across the deck
of the lakehouse with the deck.

Black plum in green bowl stands for Earth
as I try to remember the taste of dirt,
beaten by bullies who inherit the earth,
and when dinosaurs roamed the earth
it didn't strike them to build out of the sod
a covering, an interior, a private Earth.
They ran snapping all over the earth,
through ferns & tar. Now turned into stones.
Emotional ancestors launch stones
until survivors sort rubble from earth,
bury kin in rectangles of soil
until vision of love is image of soil.

Lions lose shape, become pure tooth, at night.
Disfigurement is one of night's obligations,
and the soul can become disfigured at night
as well as the body. I have spent all night

hanging on this drainpipe, lost from my body.
Maybe I've been changing slowly all night
as the moon passed over your chimney, as night
told its dim stories where half of sorrow belongs,
heart attack, taxicab, or fire belongs,
belonging to invisible gunships firing at night.
I almost forgot my body. The radio plays soul.
The market trades a black plum for each soul.

Black plums fall from pockets in your dress
and roll like near thunder across the stage.
You billowed in clouds instead of a dress,
but no hurricane warning is fierce as your dress,
nor shakes the heart with its mildred drum.
Beginning dancers may imagine an absolute dress
that binds the dance to whoever wears the dress,
like Orpheus winding the world around his guitar.
The dancer is unable to go on despite the guitar,
its grief not cobbled together by the dress,
last dance for this round of dancing,
this topple-forward war-tear of dancing.

To be sure, I'm asking around for wool.
That's why I'm calling, in order to go on.
My mistress can only make love on a bed of wool,
so I'm trying to lay my hands on as much wool
as my hands can carry before the dawn
offers up loneliness and undimpled wool.
I'm desperate, baby. No arguing with wool.
She says it's the finest touch ever made.
Concern for fineness is not American-made.
No one will help out this poor fool.
Already I see her leaving, and the way she walks
consigns me to prattle on the catwalks.

My mistress could teach how fortune's turned
away from delight, to project the unexpected,
its grabbery. Blackjack tables are overturned.
The deck chairs are overturned.
Look for more when you run out of thread,
count on more than four aces in a deck.
At night a cartoonishness paces the deck
looking for residual icebergs of oblivion.
I walked beside the captain, debating oblivion,
the ways we pictured it. Quiet on the deck.
A figure snoozed against a lifeboat turned
upside down for shade. The captain turned

and told me kings go mad and dine on soil
when their soldiers run out of stones,
that the poor go somewhere else to cut sod
and measure their rectangles of dirt,
that this is it, spaceman: life on Earth,
this dancing, my dancing, her dancing.
I wish my body would become a guitar,
when my soul is just beginning to drum
the lines that separate self from stage.
Crossed, they ghost the body a dress.
Failure's no problem for one who walks
without destination. The promise I've made
is to stay glad every dawn,
with one moment enough to go on,
shorn from time's fullest wool,
though its fabric is sometimes returned
and exchanged for cheaper oblivion,
preferring with its infinite thread
the confusion that reigns on deck
when repetition wearies the soul,
though its fabric sometimes belongs

tucked tight across my sleeping body
as my soul slips away from obligations
and steps outside to glare at the night.

Little Song

To leave you is like waking, or refusing to wake,
in that way the body has of haunting itself.

Returned to your hand, I'm the astronomer
unable to lower his telescope, or look away.

You're the telescope, too. Close, you show me
far reaches that are themselves not even the beginning.

Not to be the one who left is to live in an alarm.
The unstraightened bed.

But don't I always bring bright souvenirs from our travels,
a feather, a coin, a bee? Astonishing in my palm.

Minutes past your touch, what our bodies were
is disappearing like a ship caught in polar ice,

covered up, compressed into deep. To leave you
is where the icicles fall, the fog we wake to.

Inland Empire

Up late reading zombie
comic books, I wake
to first-person shooters
and coffee in the red mug
Jeffie left behind when she
moved back to Hammond.
My disarray is so local.
The pilot light's gone
the way of all lost pilots
into the dark waters
of the Whirlpool furnace.
And yet I find myself
strangely hopeful, eating
the three hard-boiled eggs
Jill made before her long
drive through the burn
to San Bernardino, origin
of Hell's Angels,
McDonalds, and Zappa.
It's 11:11, time
to make my daily wish,
catch the stilt legs of those
two birds who land twice
a day inside the clock.

Ragged and high
and weird and in need,
who reach deep for grief,
high for sorrow,
who work for that effect,
what effect seems unlabored,
who phrases the fingerprint,
the ironworks,

the fatal asunder,
I admire, stumblingly,
in ways that make me dive
all the way to the bottom
of the idea. What I don't say
anymore, I say in fall,
to various people in a paper,
leaf-like tradition
who remember in falling leaves
various people, while I keep trying
to lose you, in my fashion,
failed and constant.

Recent Changes at Canter's Deli

The telephone is no longer upstairs.
Cut fruit in cold cup will never be whole.
Nothing is where it was. The plate
is beside the bowl. My mind's all fucked up,
distorted, pale light reflected on stainless steel
of the walk-in cooler. It is not where it was.
Here's the spike to build a body of receipt.
Sweat collects on the waterpitcher lip
like the goodbye of a woman I loved.
The clerk bends his body to pray the miracle
of the handwashing station, turns knife to loaf.
The present pours into the pepper shaker.
It settles on the silk ivy of the now. Odds fade
in the sports section fallen between the counter,
where paying my bill I orphan a dime
for a silver mint, and the window snows sun
brilliant on Fairfax, demanding the commute.
They are not letting me drive anymore
and turning onto Melrose on the bus,
the driver, I overhear, has another job,
one he doesn't know the name for.
Up in the haze some undiscovered animal
watches us, its plan mapped out, fire
swinging up the canyons, unfolding
until flame may flicker tip of sabertooth fang
in the museum where rare finds are hidden.
I, too, am a dinosaur. Rawr. My little claws.
I'm the dredge flopping for tar from the pits.
Click. I am a kind of David Bowie
in the Amoeba everything's-a-dollar bin.
I have four fingers and a thumb on my right hand,
equal representation on the left, and fourteen

billion toes. I'm a windup rooster. Who I am
and what I feel are irrelevant enough to be central
to the project of contemporary American poetry.
Or perhaps any art. Poetry's just the form
of unimportance I teach teenagers above L.A.
under slanted windows that kill, by surprise,
the birds we then write about, gathering bonfire
around the small corpses, because it's cold here.

Pier Life

This morning on the municipal fishing pier
the homeless are filming a movie on the stairs

called lunch, featuring dried fish. I only mention
Marines because there are so many of them.

In the water, surfers in black wetsuits sit on boards
among the blue-green, reaching kelp.

A cormorant surfaces beside the line one ties
to his ankle to keep track of himself.

They steer into the wave to stay deep,
almost asleep on their boards.

Each seems like a man at a desk.
They look like several alphabets.

The next wave seethes them to shore.
It is deep enough to freeze, cold to drown.

Water gulfs around the pilings, brushes my shadow
against barnacles that remind the pier of its decay.

Cormorants climb out of the dark cellar.
If you were delicious, they would dive after you

with powerful small webbed feet or leave only a feather.
The problems of language are mostly solved

in the fish's gutting on the public sink, and thrown to sea
lions by the old woman with fierce embarrassment for a hat.

A girl staring at a croaker cut in half
runs to daddy. She reminds me that terror

has a place here, in the beginning, among strange messages.
An angler casts seven hooks that shine like carnival beads.

The ocean may not have a center but here are its margins.
Soon this attention will be over and I'll return to car,

wheel baby across the difficult tracks,
the ice in my soda barely melted.

Like Night Catching Jackrabbits in Its Barbed Wire

For my birthday we drive up the bajada
to Pioneertown Lanes, where the singer Cat Power
has left her scoresheet on the wall.
We bowl under pink and green lights.
Back in civilian footwear we walk
sand to Pappy and Harriet's Pioneer Palace,
deal Quiddler to the roadhouse *G-l-o-r-i-a,*
and then a Marine, Band-Aid on his nose,
stumbles, steals my beer. I snatch it back.
The soldier's buddy apologizes, says
forty weeks in sandbox, and they're getting him
good and drunk. An officer, my age, in slacks,
leans in to say don't worry, he's watching.
But I've been beaten up by soldiers before.
I know how certain and nearly good
fists feel when the flesh is hungry for touch.
We finish our game, the bar closes,
and those who are sober go to bed,
while those who are left drive to town,
Joshua Tree, half an hour through last
summer's forest fire, until we find
the saloon by the motel where Gram Parsons
died twice, in 1973. The first time, his hooker
expertly shoved a cube from the ice bucket
up his ass, restored him, and yet
he knew enough of life to shoot up again.
It's hard to save your own life, to take
such extreme measures alone. The woman
at the saloon, heavy with heavy curls,
collect drinks and asks *are you a Marine?*
and I do feel underwater, undersea
five thousand feet above its level
in the entangled, ragged arms

of the Joshua tree, which is a lily,
and when I wake from drowning,
beyond the Pioneertown Motel window,
the mountains are still deciding what to wear.
My wife pours orange juice into a green glass
beside black crumbs of birthday cake.

And the Yellow Bones of the Parking Lot

Snow closed the city and left my officemate
stranded in the wasteland of the key card
five long icicle days in the breakroom.
As much of what made me leave Seattle
as made me find my way back in the dark
is his story, the coyote he watched dart
into the bulldozed field for holiday rabbits
between the Microsoft and the Nintendo,
what forms of survival, what warm sodas
and granola he scavenged from unlit drawers,
bowl of Caesar salad some project manager
ordered before the storm and he found wilted
in a conference room, fallen in like a grave.

Perhaps on your last day in Seattle
you will get to chase the cat, as I did,
along Northgate apartment shrubs
shared with a dentist's office, and you too
will be the fool reclining patients watch
from blue chairs and from numb faces;
the cat wants to stay, a clawed want that hides
despite the frenzy of your hands, your mad
hollering silenced by inch-thick glass.
The Northgate Theater sign reads: *Titanic*.
Beyond: the patient lifeboats of Licton Springs.
Above: the gray pinstripe suite of the late sky.

I think the bookstores are emptier now
than when at 24 I rode the 242
across the floating bridge, dreaming of sturgeon
rounded from roaming the lake's deep vowel,
a depth that unfolds like the road that brought me,
beneath light rain rhythmic on windshield.

And the cherry, apple, and plum in my yard
still ripen, do so on rough, hungover bark.
Above: a bat has spent all evening turning
over loops that trace their figures murky,
and although the home I left was always gone
and the one I will never catch I keep in mind,
the bat will go on however it wants to.

West Coast

Mike's up from Noe Valley one Friday
and we go out to Copper Gate
in Ballard with his in-laws, for pickled
herring and strange Danish cheeses.
Decorating the restaurant bathroom
hang light boxes displaying nude
women posing in black-and-white,
and men who are dressed like women.
This used to be a sailor's bar, and what
remains is this form of their loneliness,
and it becomes mine for a few hours,
reminding my body of its lusts
for close skin and how different from light
skin is, more like glass, or the breathing
of a horse in a dark, sodden field.
We split off from the group to ramble
the provincial streets, wander bookstores
in and out, bars, a burger stand.
Kansas is a cold dessert, I say.
No Kansas is a tongue depressor, he says.
You can't speak freely. The aquavit
we drink is clear as the rust of stars,
and my mind is shaped like a prow,
all black wood and forward riding.
When we return to Copper Gate
the only light remaining is above the grill,
a thin tube like a line in a play.
We're still up, walking the streets,
looking for ketchup for the fries
Mike has discovered in his jacket,
and we are trying to remember which kid
it was at the pool hall back in Topeka

who bragged he could bend his body
and kiss his own penis, and showed us
I think in the alley, but Mike says no,
not the kid who could pop out his eye
made of glass, and let you handle it
for a dollar, but Cliff, who knocked
Mike down after a basketball game,
for winning, and he never showed us.
Our high-minded speculation fades
as we try to find the car, remembering
only that it faced the ship locks,
and when we find it we eat the fries
cold, and let the paper bag be taken
by the wind along the water, and settle
onto its currents, among the rustling gulls.

Pilgrim: An Ode

I'm due back any minute.
Only the shape I arrived in is left.
The curator paces.
I have no choices. One
has no choice. It is

a fixèd thing. The world
falters. But unaware my twin
goeth about his same hour
in sweats, manning the rummage sale

in the year's first weather.
It doesn't budge. I cannot
it alter. My anguish holds fast

as oak limb to earth, here,
or any hinge, in the face
of which I loosen and fray.

*

Sneakers carry tons of teenaged sissies
past acceptance, running laps around our
less imagined selves. We spring from asphalt,
masculine adults with reasonably
priced conveyances, these normal dudes now.

Buy cigars and sell them back to Carlo.
"Avalon" was challenged by Puccini.
No one thought to copyright the whooping.
Daytime drunks unnerve me with their yodels.
Only servants' oils soothe me now.

Half of you, who love me, will deceive my
lover on our journey over hillocks,
river levees, valley tightropes, castle
moats, and also, even sleeping, photo
album pages flip your wintry bridges.

Catalogues made sisters mourn, escaping
forests filled with model-sharing mirrors
they could *be,* one summer hour, after
shadows crisped the pool. This tidy jumper
settled over smaller risqué swimwear.

Black, as ink is king, and long as hands are,
bought in bulk along with bully daggers,
I would not contemn its source nor dozy
find my fault with my productive whatnot.
Part is false, but also heaven, partly.

*

I saw you. Bus 74
from Bay City to Harbor View:

red ribbons, sword-short ears
like Mickey Mouse in high dudgeon.
Am I wrong or did our eyes meet?
Admit the sweetness there. Box 242.

*

I saw you.
Lecturing on Spinoza, eighth row back,
fourth seat in. Two buckets hath

mine Globetrotter,
one filled with glitter,
the other,
water.

*

Who's *not* tired of choosing between
invisibility and flight?

*

What the stains from our last get-together
spelled in Rorschach, or manifesto,
only bleach can read. Its spray bottle
dissolves from life what living cannot hold,
leaching fabric back to new, each thread loved.

After the show they tear the curtain down,
spread it like night across the stage, and fold it.
Hands at each corner make a fast loop
through the air and trap the edges
so the curtain's flesh falls into its body,
a bundle they take into the back
until the next time something's over.

Mister Skylight

When you enter the city of riots, confess

what turns your life has taken,
what is hard-on and what is mineral. Confess
until the wind catches itself by the tail.

Or find some solace. Mr. Skylight captains
a houseboat downstream like a vitamin.

I can only just begin to bear the chain-link fence.
Reflected in a puddle, the image trembles
as I tremble. The image freezes, I shiver.

It is like the enormity Gregor Samsa
is hoping to sleep through, but, well, can't.

The woman playing Atari in public has, has...
Everything's hauled away. In buckets.

These peaches, for example. I have heard
of you, yes, the monkey says. The moon
offers its offensive and ridiculous bulge.

Out in the salvage yard the snowy drifts

are not snow. White paint on frames,
they lean against front doors that won't open in.
Mr. Skylight, stumbling through, asks

"Didn't we just finish painting this wall?
Aren't the brushes still drying on the sill?"

When the moment opens again,
remember to feel the immense province
pulling in, a hand here and here,

remember to smell what first was sweet,
apricots just sliced, one half-globe still rolling.
His wife ran upstairs to call police

as the "assailant took the victim's own
paring knife from the counter."

We show this on the snowy channels
most sets veil, between the black and white:

how they dragged Mr. Skylight inside and made
demands, then went deeper into his building,

and the iron gate lifted off its spindle.

Hill of stubble in moonlight, the hog

bristles across the lawn,
eats whole bouquets, eats bouquets whole,
plowing tusk through silk rose, a fresh lily.

Our headstones surrender their salt.
Wilder animals would not perturb us.
Worse hogs will cross and sand

down names. This one, at least, grunts life.
He would eat hog, could he make one die.

If there is a man inside the hog costume,
wanting to feel unchanged, so there is a hog
wearing an interior fake man.

When I tell Mr. Skylight my dream

he doubles my prescription. Pen in hand,
he gestures at his shelf of resources
and says *take your pick*. At the same moment,

your butcher jabs his butcher knife
toward the row of basted ham shanks,
take your pick.

We leave the dock at dawn for trout.
What Argonauts we are.

Dawn-lavendered boats bring in night's catch.
I stand above in the gray sweatshirt,
belly full of cauliflower soup,

in a light rain. On the sidewalk, a

teenager repairs a
satellite with a wrench.

I never go to town, but go ahead, please.

Town's for those who care for being seen.
I have this mirror to magnify my flame,

a funhouse glimpse. When I don't see it
I'm ghost. It's true I've become stone.

Awake, I see *their* lights in return; asleep

on the walkway I feel their immense dreams,
from crow's nest to captain's quarters.
They chart their paths. I rudder my continent,

which I'm still learning. You try, Skylight.
I've fashioned this wheel. It attaches at the eyes.

A bellow from the soccer stadium,

musty, erotic, indignant,
lands against my brick wall
and rolls through the broken window.

I hear what it says: *be alone.*

As the roaring emerges into a chant
naming the home team.

It is more like marriage than
marriage is, this town at dawn.

How streets seem to turn,
continue under a new name,
reverse, are plowed up

for reconstruction.
In an unfinished apartment,
worklights silhouette

the sawhorse and the sander
left out for the morning shift.

Stumbling toward the kitchen
I switch the darkness off,
disturbing a triangle moth who,

thinking perhaps that night
has moved into my black T-shirt

flutters toward me and clings
with undovelike feet.

I am the fifth son of a lawyer

from the American Midwest.
I know my circumstance.

I come from the gun and the whip.
From the ox that pulls forward.
The Conestoga, the Cessna engine.

The first satellite was carved on a whale ship
in 1822, out of New Bedford, and hung

by my grandfather leaning on his stepladder,
which we still own. My father was

the inventor of the joke, in 1958,

in Paris doing backbends for the lodge,
standing on a crate of gin,
a stadium blanket around his shoulders.

Now September, a banjo
hanging from an attic hobnail.

Hole in an attic.

The river drowns boys who guess wrong.

Eats whole towns. Eats towns whole.
Oak, shark, mansion, whale,

and each mountain that has dared to rise.
I cannot see the words I am thinking.

Looking up, past the water fountain,

I see the Superdome, poached egg
where the Saints play. Some men with ropes
climb the curve, hose whitewash down.

Mr. Skylight lights a Bulgarian cigarette
and reclines while the other men work.

Knowing suddenly how, I sing along.
I, too, am tired of miraculous recoveries,
the *mono no aware* of survival,
these supple cancers disappearing

like green jerseys into the skate park.

I had forgotten that I had forgotten. I

had one hand in one century's big finish,
a new kind of metal, a bionic art:

it's a story my mother tells, thinking
of the wrong boy. She is old now.
And these stories will be forgotten
umbrellas in the coat check.

Standing on an oil rig looking north
at my country, I watch cigarettes
glow from boats passing in the dark.

On the beach, to make love, the man
and the woman step off the island.

He stares back at land. She, the sky.

A fat fish, days dead, washes up. Crabs
scuttle from the side, pick it clean.

On the exact dune where he fixes his edge,
when he does, a scribbled indecipherment
scrawls vine through the sand. She

navigates by the stars, by Sirius,
the dog. She recognizes her collaborator,

the dizzying recombinations.

Windy again on the lakefront last night.

We're getting our own apartment.
Rolled out of bed about one ten.
Pissed off, I said *I don't think so.*

Sunlight has so little tenure.
He flew out and was hit by a propeller.

The little man, you mean? The boy.
He had fever. I couldn't take him.

But I have always hewed to that music made
from gentle modifications,
the lake-effect modulations

provoked into motion and never
the frame-frozen getaway.

And I said *Donald.* You *can not*
hold him all the time. You got to
put him down sometimes.

No one could find the right shoes on sale.

The chancellor ferried the study subjects
and set them loose, armed them with steak knives.
After carving up the painting faculty, they began
this serious and important work.

The lights are going down. Your mother stands
at the door, her check for our visit

sweaty in her hand. But I have more to teach.
Listen as I take my paint from this vein
and trace the ocean's dissolve,

dissolve myself and my voice
(at my peril)
                untie the rendezvous

sleeping city

Stand here.

Each night we are sentenced to reenact
Gloucester falling blind off Dover.
Travel + Leisure runs a list of hotels

catering to the nightly panorama,
yet elsewhere, too, he falls

like snow over the union bars
of Minneapolis while the Vikings lose,

windowless drug treatment centers
in Winnipeg and Regina and Kelowna,

he falls and falls and his son never says,
as the son is obligated to say, fall

harder, accumulate, close the schools,
spend all white day in the ecstasies.

Ah, send the essential workers back to bed
and suffering that brings them
to keep working on the renovations,

painting of a marsh, whose every wandering
off the canvas into the music

comes from the paint-plastered radio
whose plug droops into the dropcloth.

Big shot walks up his hat atilt,

a knife fight in his instep, starts laying it on.
The sky falters into the gutters, lobs a few

grenades against the barn, flash and pop,
and the air smells like cat. Am I a cop?
The thought had sprung up. The DJ is half man

and the floor looks like meowing. The idiot sweats.

It chews his haunch. For years now.
Where are the tigers to replace him?

Outside Long Beach Airport,
pigeons have shat white the loudspeaker
deplaning locals roll suitcases by,

and always someone wears a pink
cowboy hat, or a fur from another climate.
Beside the boy with interlocking skulls

raining on his hoodie, the house sparrow
goes for crumbs of stale bagel.
The pilot's gold epaulets catch on the cab door.

I then am Portuguese, spying through a glass,

leafing through maps up sort of the Nile,
or am returning, my knapsack
a jumble of unbearably small jade statues.

In this pane the gray cloud
is my mother in her housecoat.

Not all craft sink. Moored in a meadow,
the yacht rose above the valley. I found it
after a long time walking alone.

The mountains had battened it down,
scratched out its name.

Any fool could see it was the ark,
sign of some survival, quiet as Ash Wednesday.
I knocked on its ribs and no one answered.

Why should I think of this now?
The park's closed. She locks the gate,

the carnival attendant, and drives home
to wash her convertible before the sun goes down.

Bring some beers over, she says.

Rain trick-or-treats the couple's door,

but it is their red sedan that has been candied.
The hood glistens like licked cinnamon.

Perhaps I am riding an ox-drawn cart
on the western dip of Cuba's green mustache.
The oxen are pulling their white thighs

across the water the rice field pours in.
The peppertrees are turned up to the highest degree.
There is a sunset, finally.

Something is over again. Unbundle the curtain,
hang it on the bar, raise it into the dusky fly.

I dig my beat, sweating. I hold out. I get taken,
who never understands my hunger, its

terrible comfort.

A hole as if Skylab has fallen

through the clouds into my disarray,
a precise pouch, precise and utter

removal, force an eye from some dark animal
all pupil, with no center. The alley

tortures.
There is a pavement to her comedy.

Mincemeat dragged through a wet glacier.
A dagger slipping across the continent's ribcage.
I am one long hear. Put your hand in my mouth,

let me taste, and in return, feel all my orbits.
You think time flies? It falls to earth.

But sometimes evenings after dinner,
the news, the pipe he knocks against the railing,
my father spoke about the time their Buick

tumbled down the hill and she was pregnant
with the first boy, how their comfort spun.

He is still surprised, each moment, how
they rose and dusted themselves off,

and, feeling the baby kick, and, the tires
having landed right, just drove home.

The late-night menu mumbles something (inaudible).

Fat roils the smoked turkey in the black skillet,
as I chop mint from Strawberry Creek,
and I am parsing onions, carving peppers,
segmenting celery and measuring flour.

Mr. Skylight shines down, full,
engorged, shining on all ships from the gorilla sky.

A laziness settles over dogs and foxes.

Get Skoog with the whale ballet in his head.
Listen, the first alarm. Man the lifeboats.
Then, as neighbors move around their house

at night, shuffling and washing,
help a man who falls in, over and over.
Now all the horses are
poplars waving across the immense field.

Jesus in my nightmare
comes down the gravel driveway,
a teenager in sportswear
go home I say
he says *give me your home.*

This is it, spaceman: life on Earth.

It starts when she turns off the lamp
and points to the city's orange crown.

Schoolchildren hold up candles
for Mr. Skylight's midnight ride.

By now I could hold it in my palm
or sip from it. From some porches,
the night is more. Get ready

for the all-skate, the group swim.
My hand falls to her lap, our teeth click.

My soul steps outside. Down boulevards
hot rods abduct the day. *Saudade*

in carwash dust; wind along a post office;
a sprinkler reflected in the windows.
The pool's open; why aren't we swimming?

On the garbage truck, the runners hang

half-out, undefined. Shouting they lift,
lug, tug, huff, drag, and push
up the bright defecations, Chinese takeout

and new Sonys, the granola salad of litter boxes,
acres of bubble wrap, ripped tissues,

fish gone bad like plague, blood clots,
suppositories, diapers, the vomit
of the cancer patient wiped up with Brawny,

rum vomit of the bright girl,

the sheet music to "Clair de lune,"
cuttings from a holly, oyster shells
on top, round mirrors of the dawn.

New Orleans, 2005

Postscript: Autobiographical

I rode my bike across the Argentine.
Marble arms rose for joy in the garden,
a slush of sculpture salvaged from wrecked ships
around Don d'Carlo's sandstone pen
carved from a boulder fallen from that cliff.

When I was a nude Sicilian youth, and had been
lounging on the piazza for a good hour,
above the sea, I heard a cry from the beach
and ran. A seal pup lay curled around
a stone. Someone—my brothers?—had beat it

senseless, so I heaved the sack of fur
back to surf, the body cooling my body,
and swam some yards until it sank to green.
Back up the steps, I dried on the wall
fell to sleep forgot the beast and grew

athletic and kept my tongue back of my head
obeyed the trainer loved a girl she climbed
a tree beside the training yard to whisper
secret names from the arbor. War grew
as we slept. I fled across the sea

to escape conjecture; I biked all over
to build a body of forgiveness, the wheels
wearing down a new world of old roads.
I rode across the Argentine, my spokes
speaking for me, to the house of a friend.

I swam in the sea there, among the mangled steel.
A lost flotilla, the hemisphere
tapped in my ear, the ticking of whales,

the warnings of sand. And when I drowned
I sank slowly and meant every fathom.

About the Author

Ed Skoog was born in Topeka, Kansas, in 1971; he graduated from Kansas State University and holds an M.F.A. from the University of Montana. After many years in New Orleans and Southern California, he now lives in Seattle with his wife, Jill Marquis, and is writer-in-residence at Richard Hugo House. He has been a Theodore Morrison Scholar at the Bread Loaf Writers' Conference and a Tennessee Williams Scholar at the Sewanee Writers' Conference. He has published three chapbooks, *Tool Kit* (1996), *L'Allegro and Il Penseroso* (2000), and *Field Recordings* (2004), and won the Poetry Prize from the Pirate's Alley Faulkner Society and the Lyric Poetry Award from the Poetry Society of America. His poems have been published in many magazines, including *American Poetry Review, The New Republic, Paris Review, Ploughshares, Poetry*, and *NO: a journal of the arts*.

The Chinese character for poetry is made up of two parts: "word" and "temple." It also serves as pressmark for Copper Canyon Press.

Since 1972, Copper Canyon Press has fostered the work of emerging, established, and world-renowned poets for an expanding audience. The Press thrives with the generous patronage of readers, writers, booksellers, librarians, teachers, students, and funders—everyone who shares the belief that poetry is vital to language and living.

Major funding has been provided by:
Anonymous
Beroz Ferrell & The Point, LLC
Cynthia Hartwig and Tom Booster
Lannan Foundation
National Endowment for the Arts
Cynthia Lovelace Sears and Frank Buxton
Washington State Arts Commission

For information and catalogs:
COPPER CANYON PRESS
Post Office Box 271
Port Townsend, Washington 98368
360-385-4925
www.coppercanyonpress.org

This book was designed and typeset by Phil Kovacevich. The text is Sabon, designed by Jan Tschichold in 1964. The titles are set in Trade Gothic, designed by Jackson Burke for Mergenthaler Linotype. The cover, title, and part titles are set in an unknown antique letterpress typeface. Printed on archival-quality paper at McNaughton & Gunn, Inc.